I0491330

Baltica

Coloring book inspired by Estonian folk art

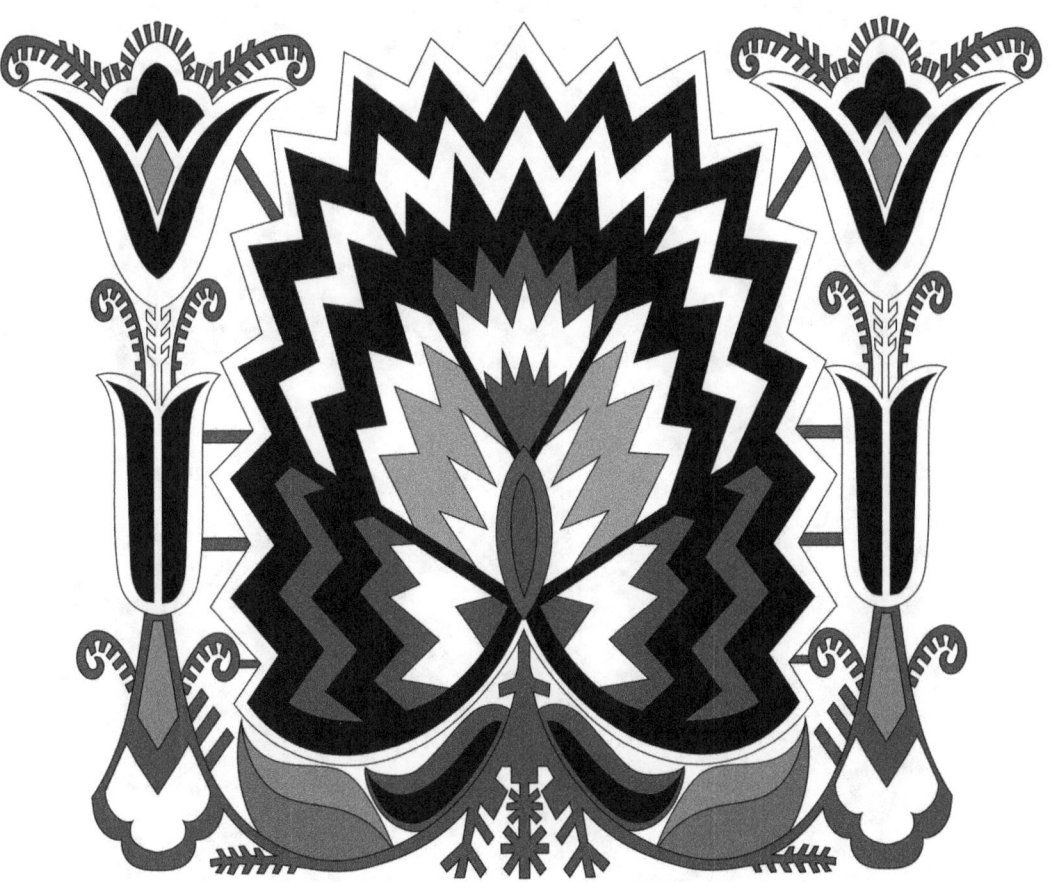

Baltica Volume IV , Second edition,

Copyright © 2025 Alice Koko. All rights reserved.

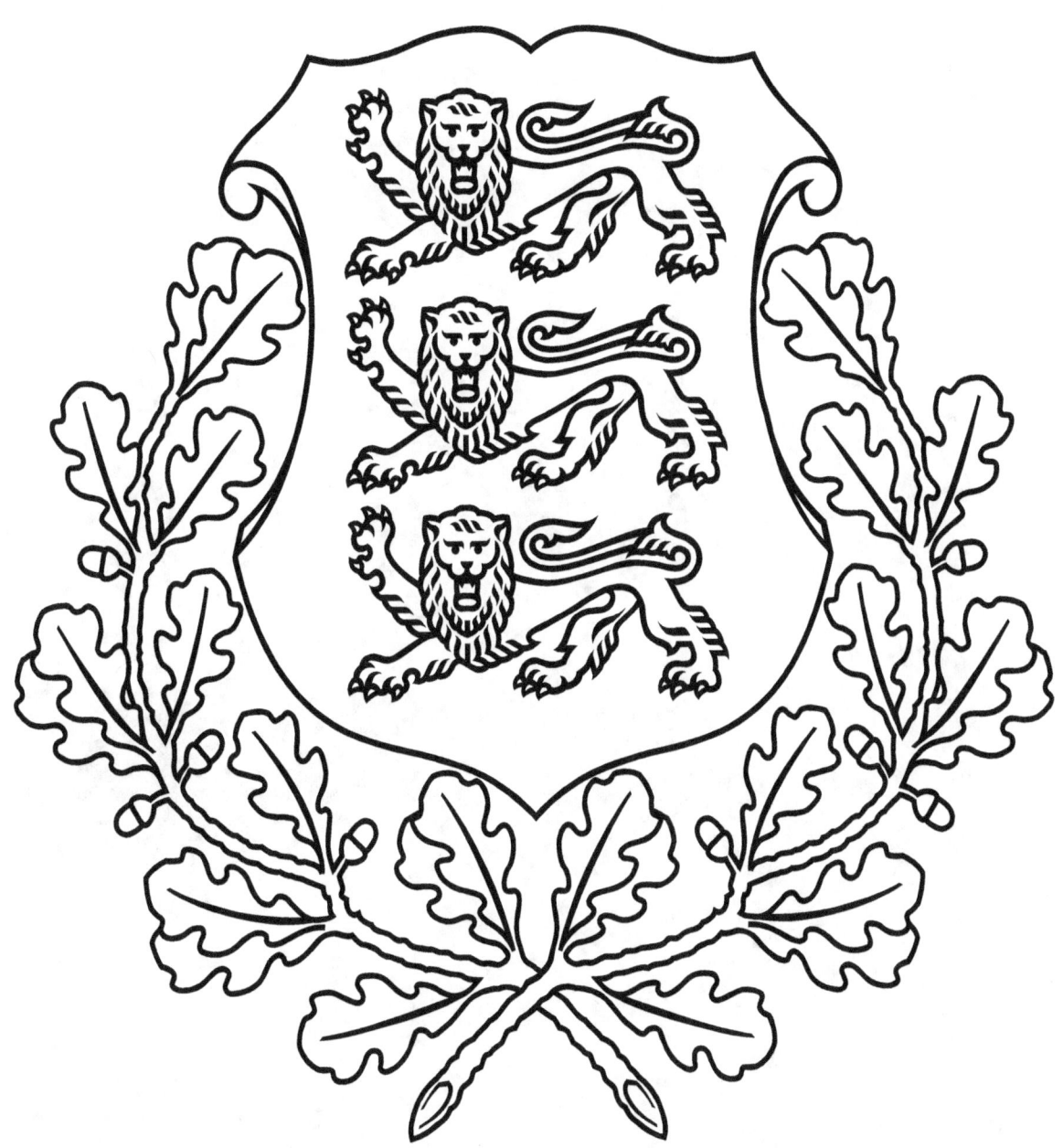

Estonia is a Baltic state in Northern Europe; having land border with Latvia
and Russia, and coastline of Baltic Sea and Gulf of Finland.
More than half of the country is covered in forests and there are 2,355 islands.
Interestingly enough, Estonia has more than one recognized capital- Tallinn
is the official one, Tartu is established as "the cultural capital of Estonia" and
Pärnu is known as "the summer capital". Tallinn is voted as the best protected
and intact medieval city in Europe.
Estonian culture is unique in its "East-meets-West" character.
Estonia is renowned for its beautiful folk art: embroidery, lace-making,woodwork and
knitwear. Cherished handicraft traditions honored and passed on for generations.
Here's a little glimpse into the beauty of the Estonian folk art.
Enjoy!

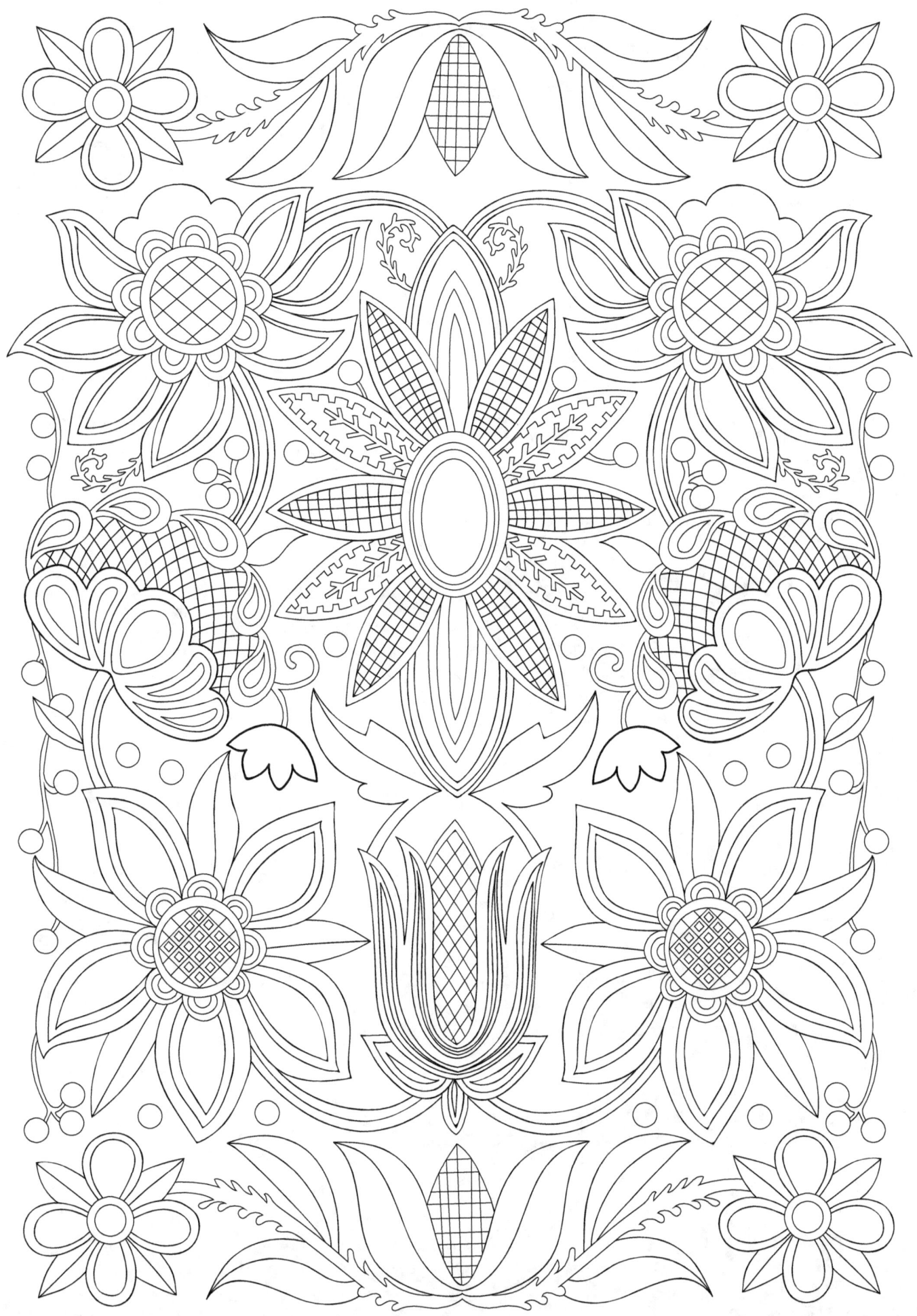

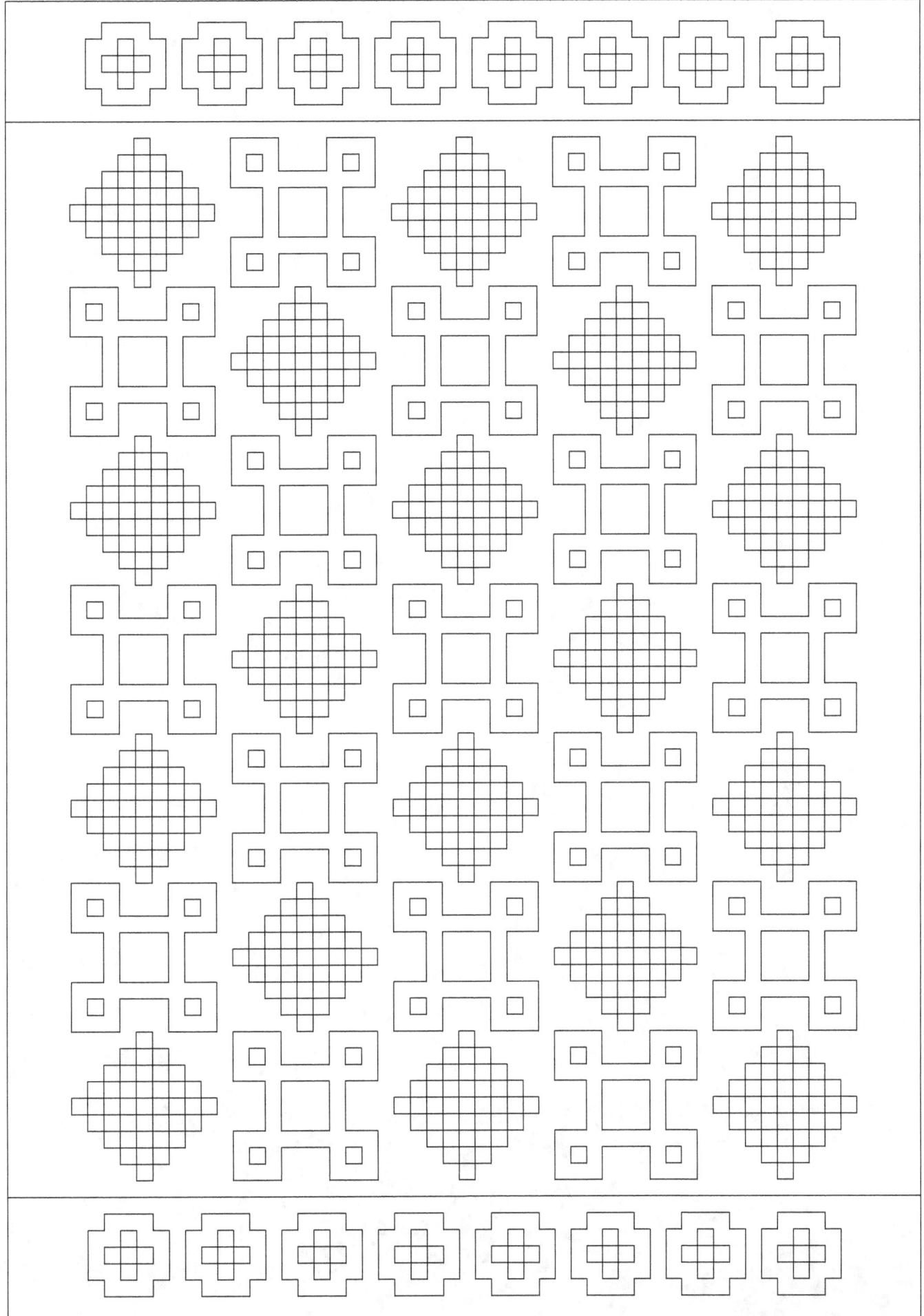

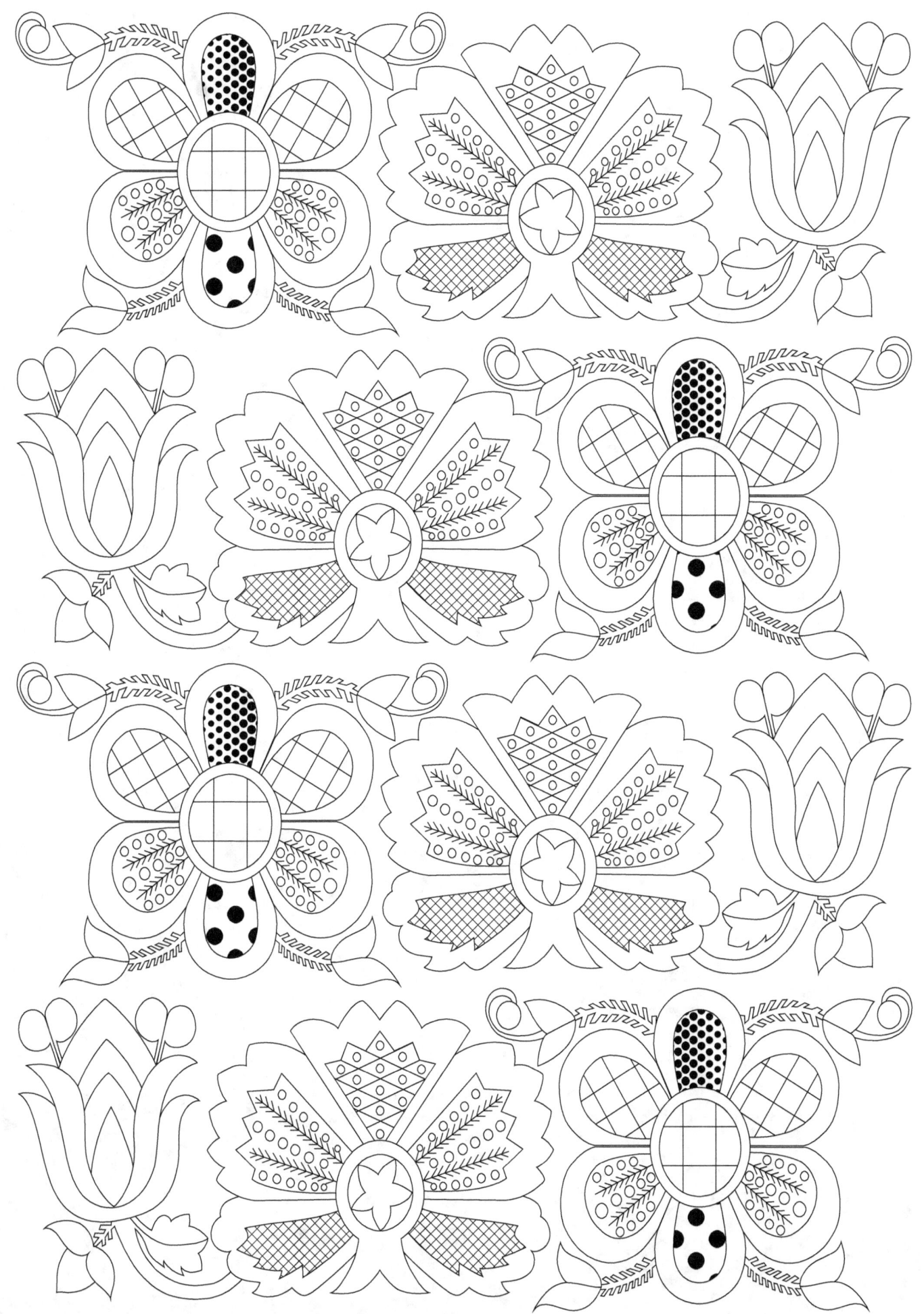

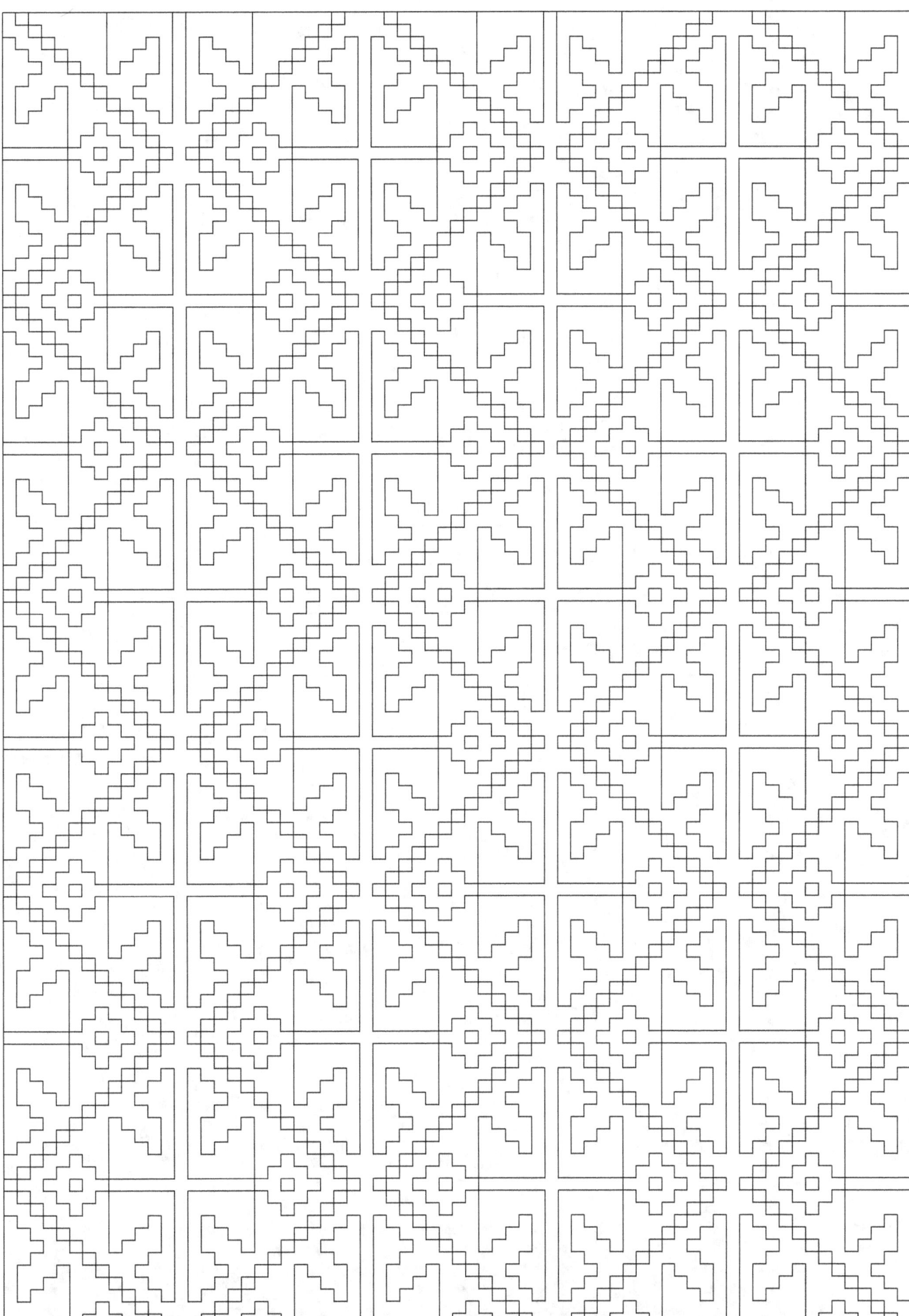

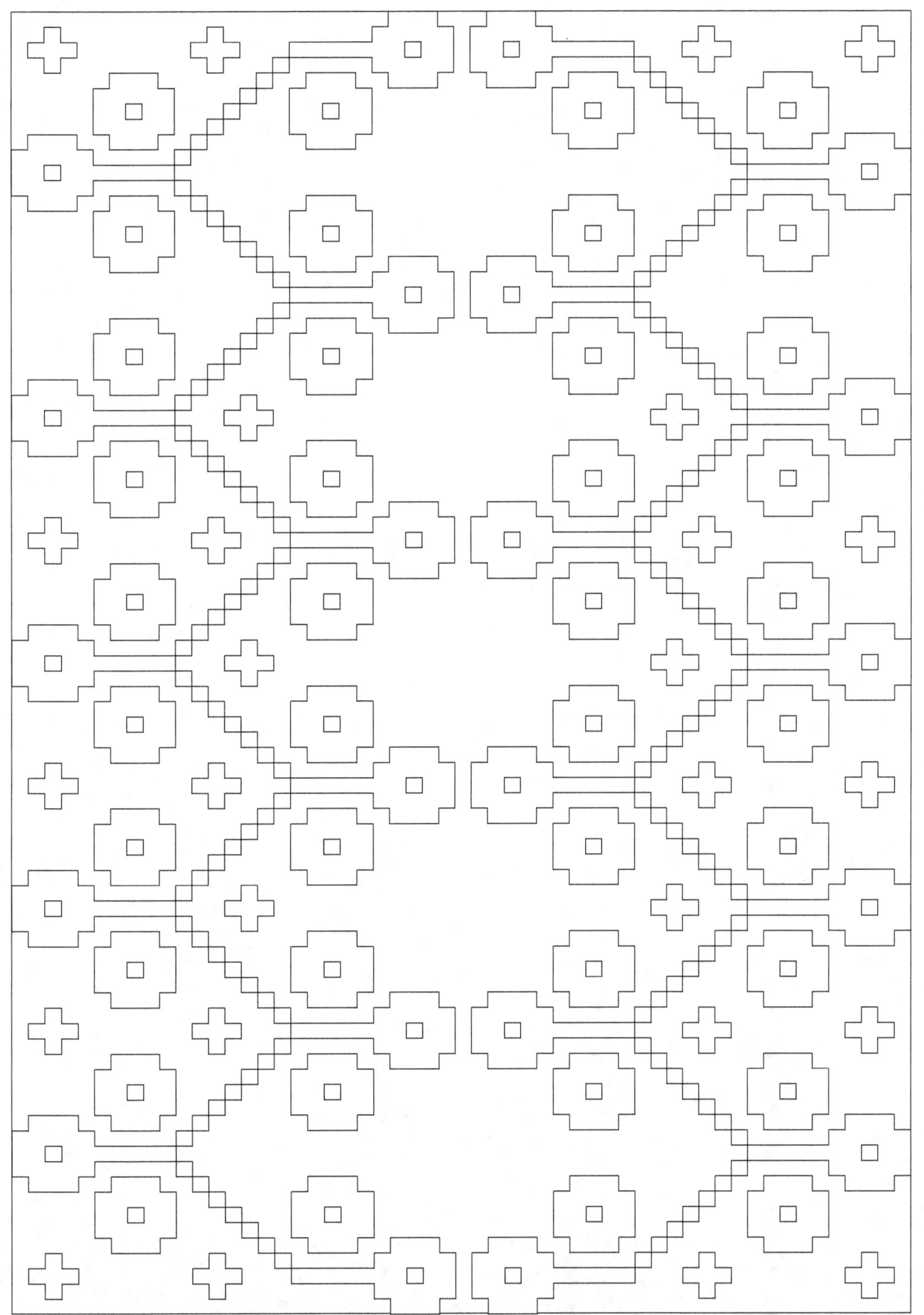

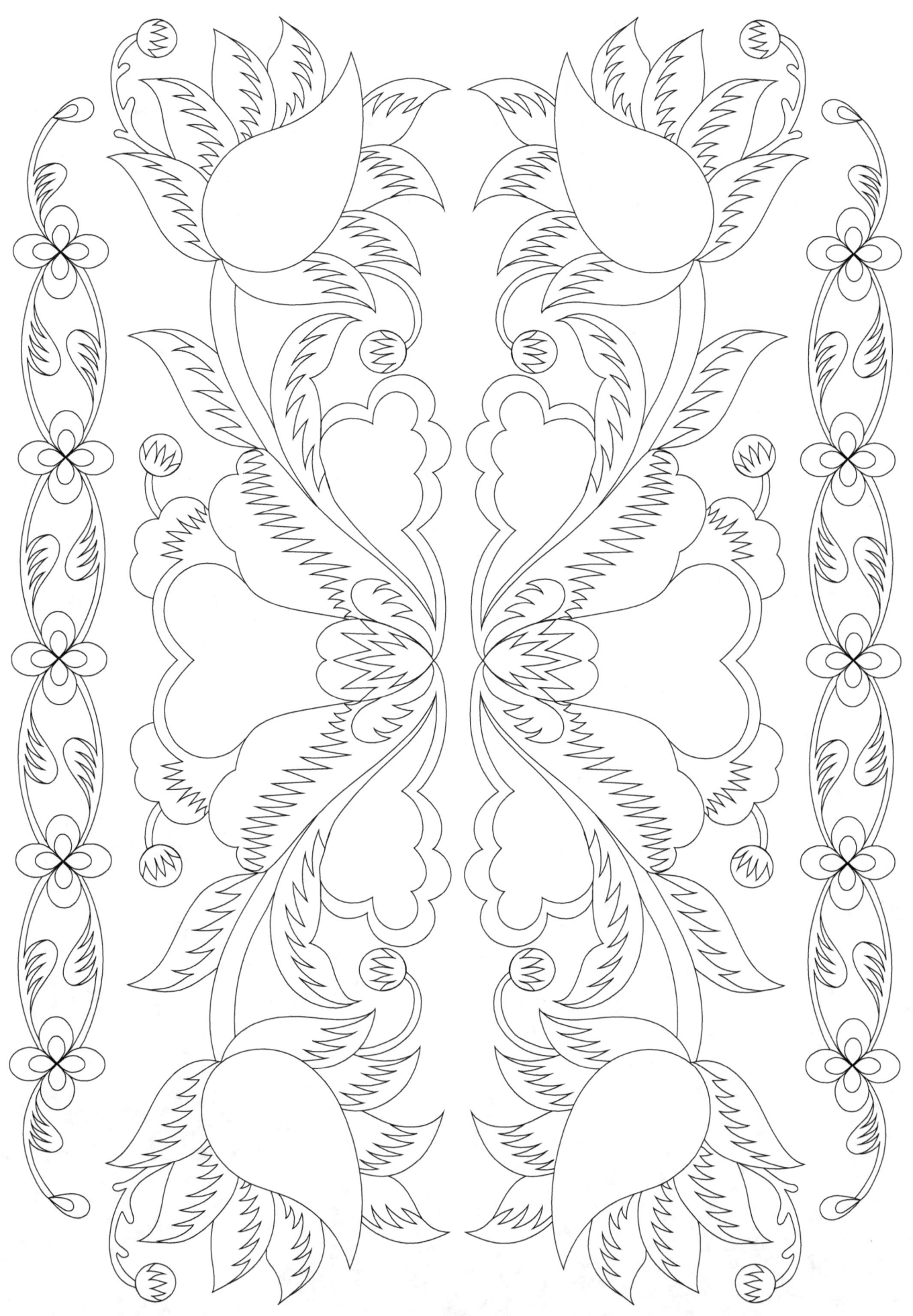

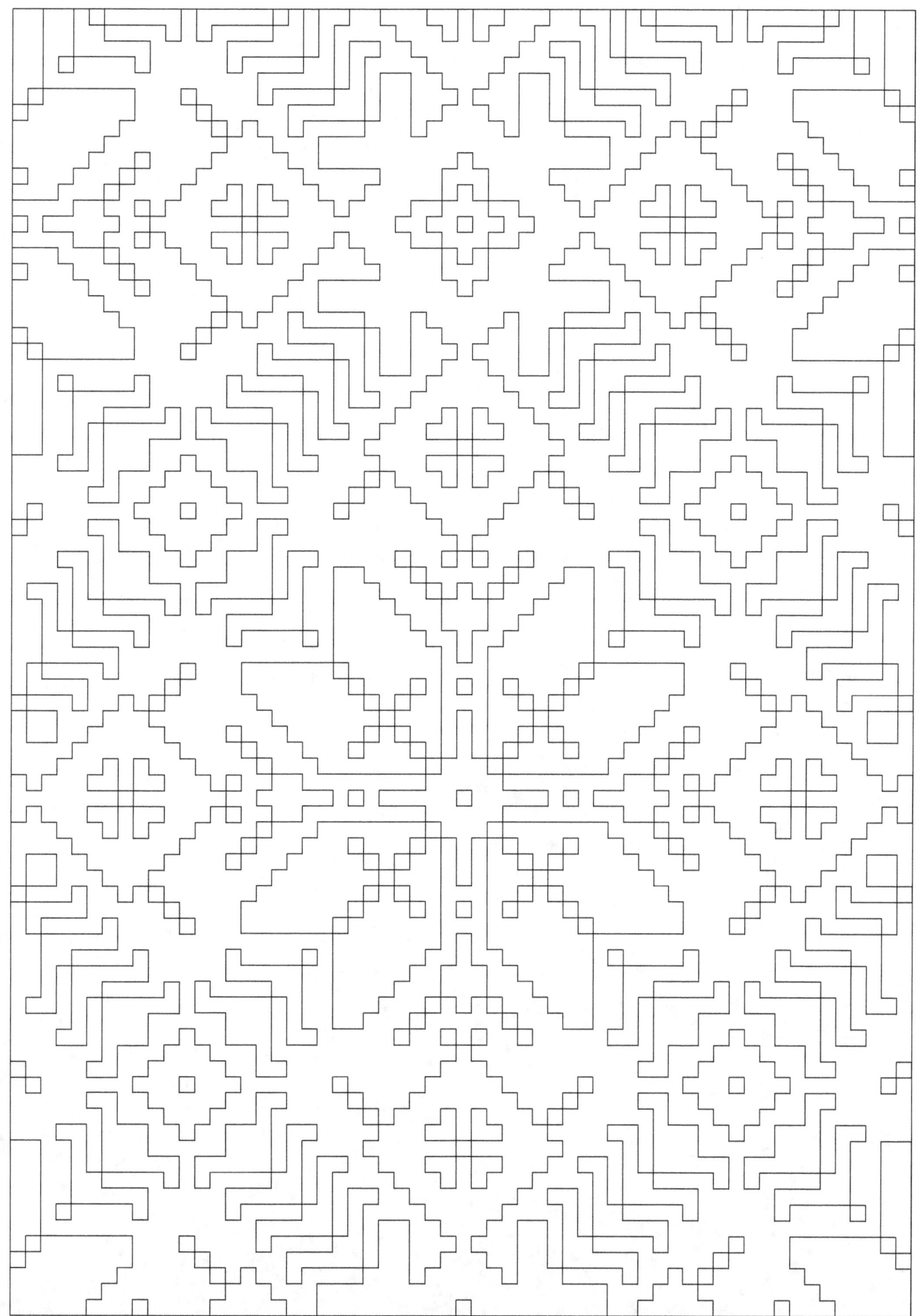

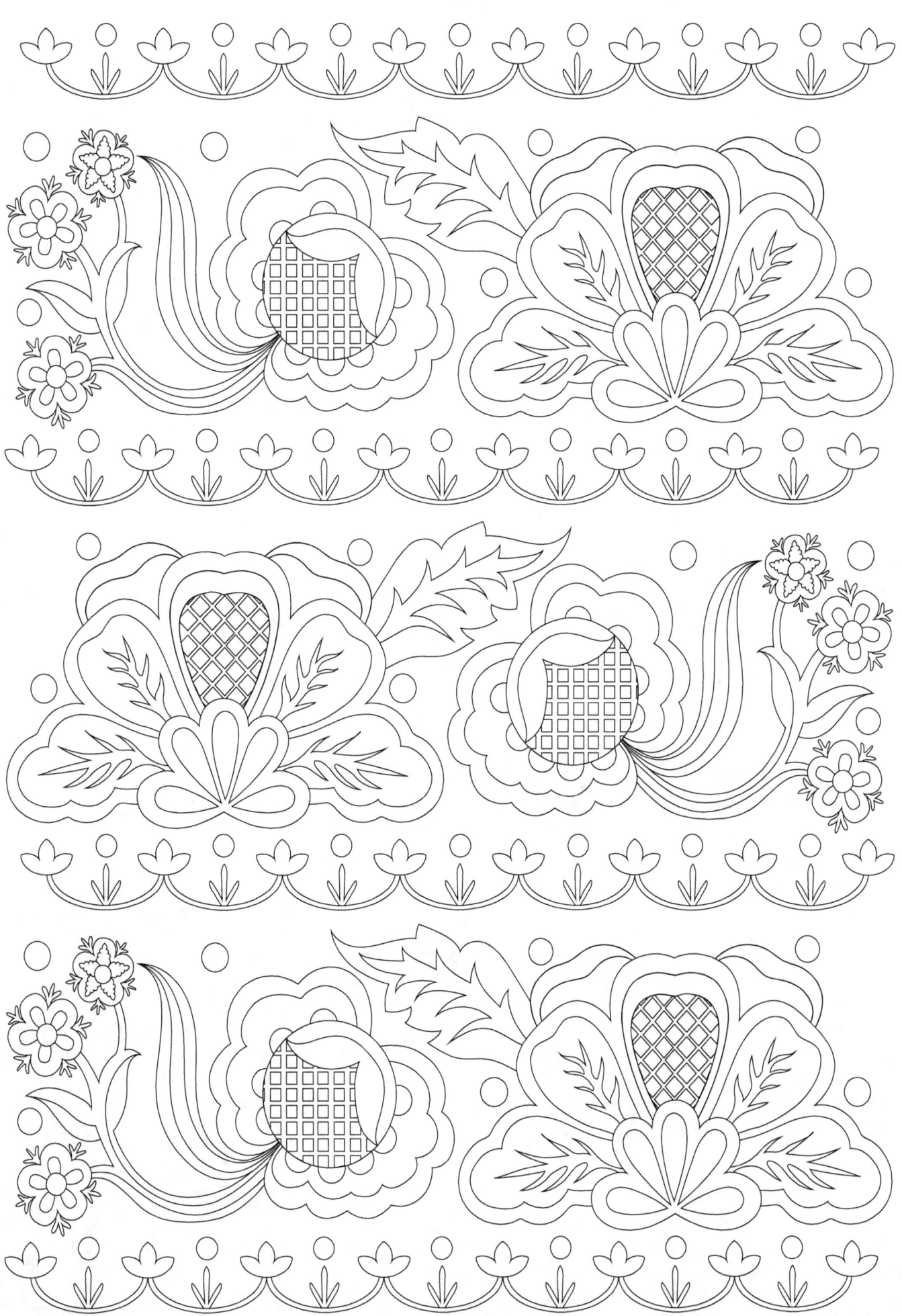

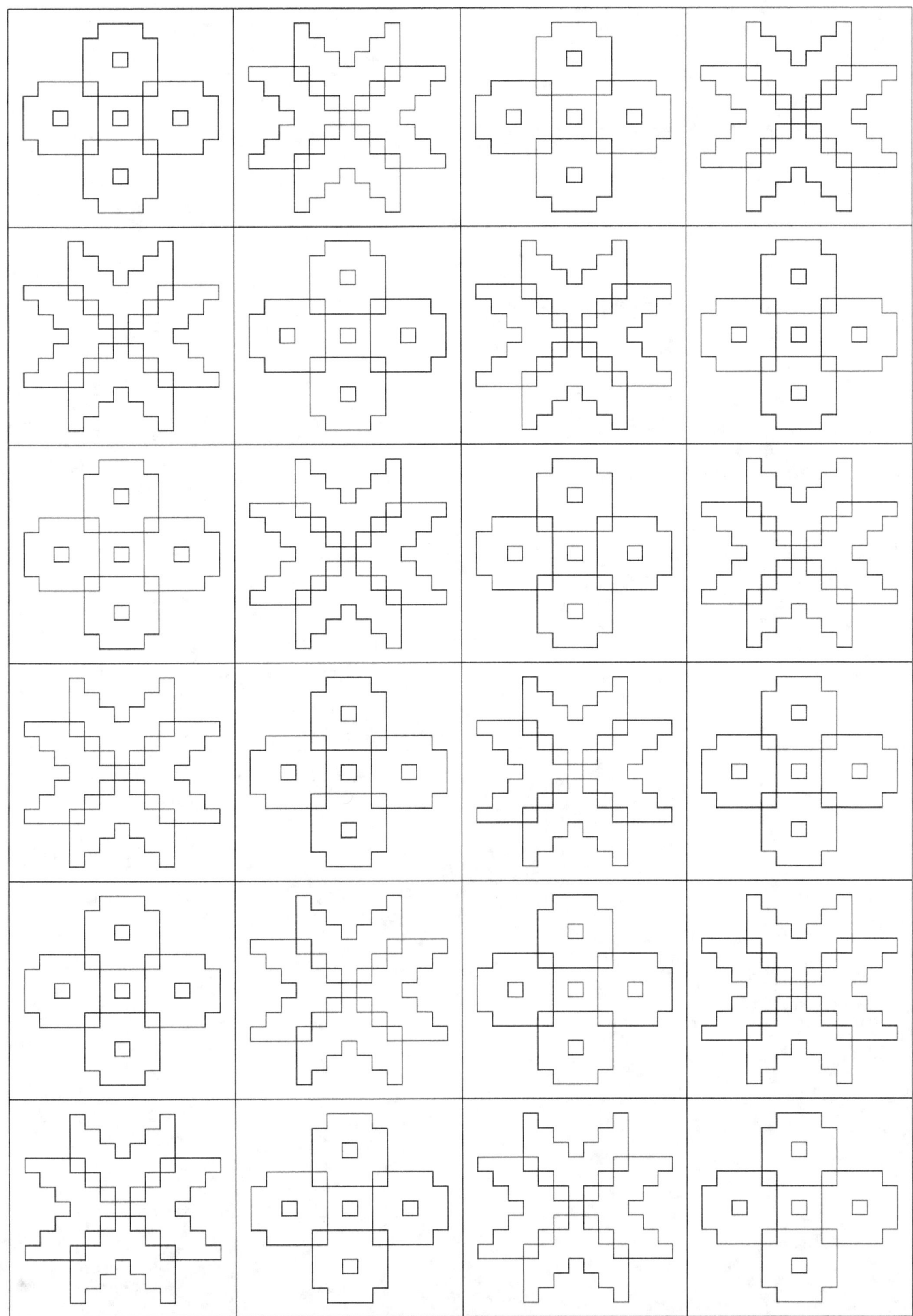

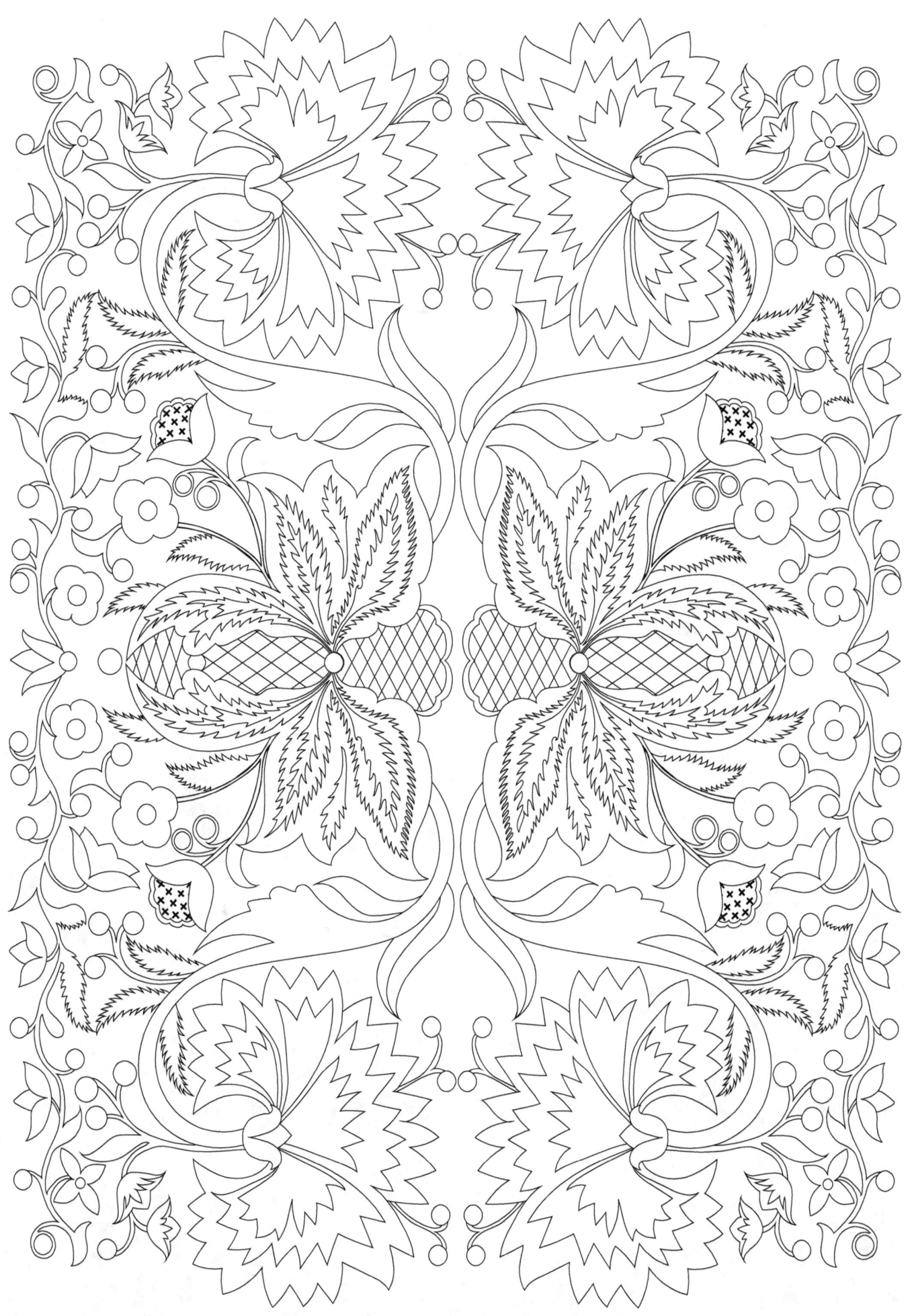

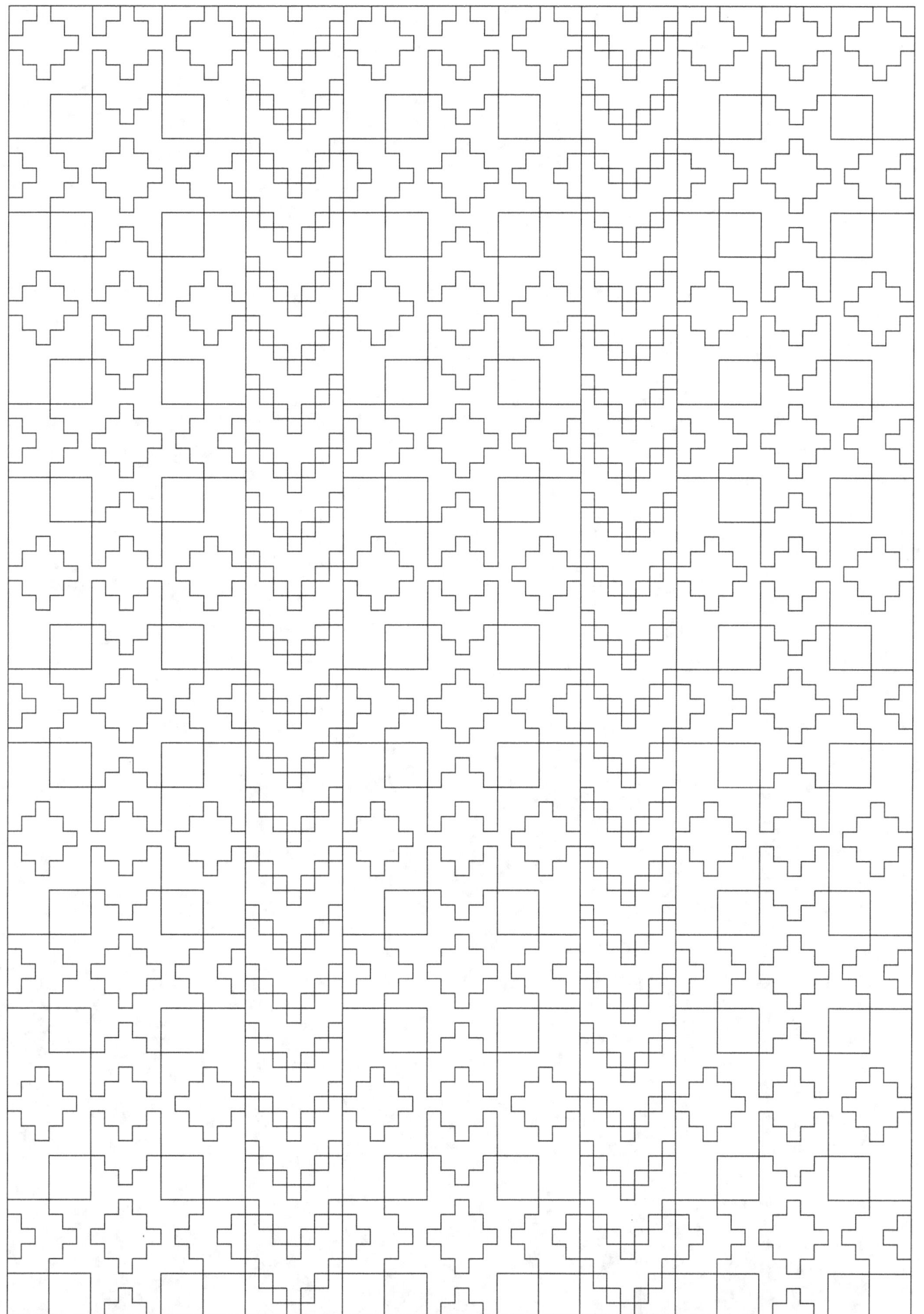

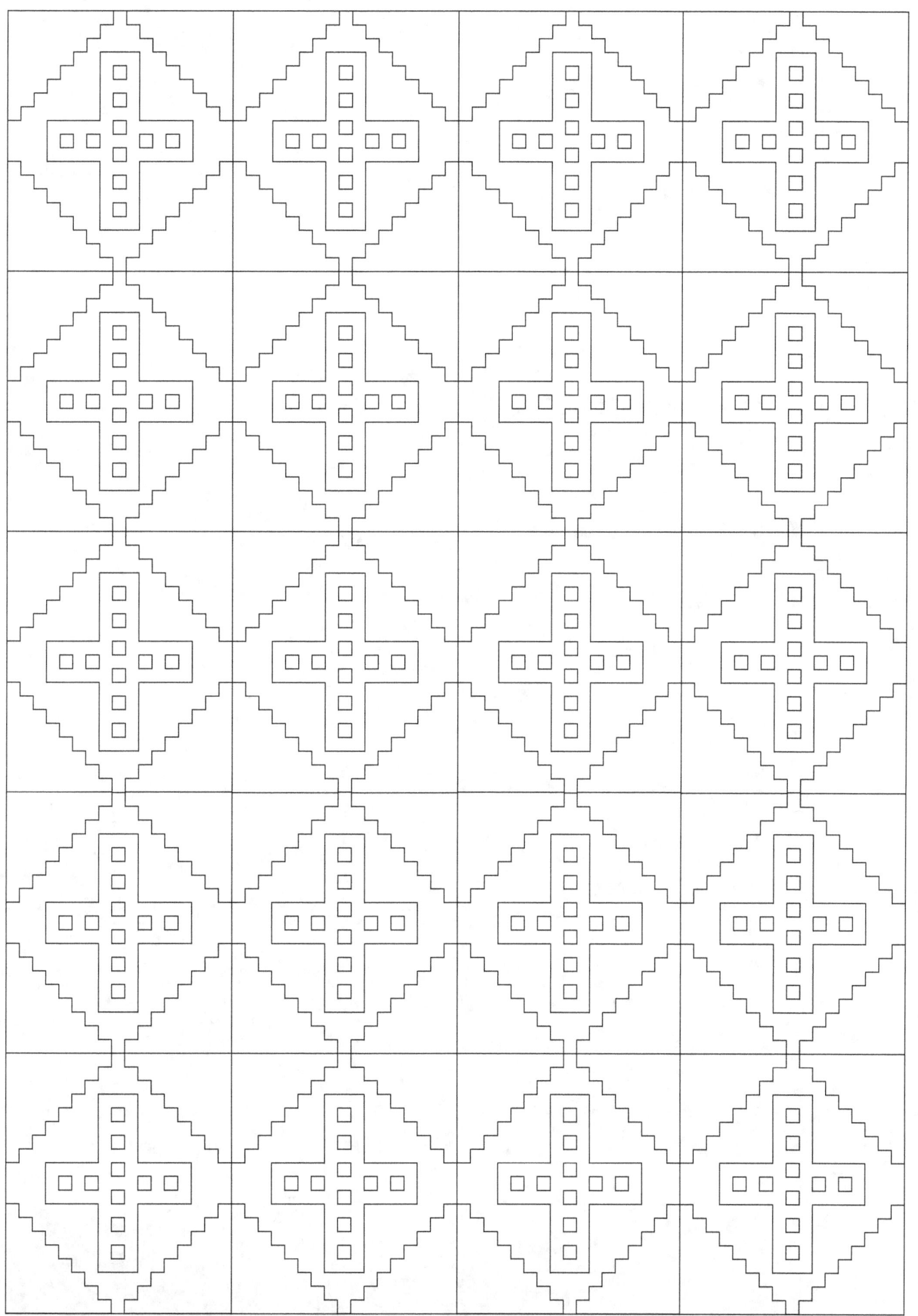

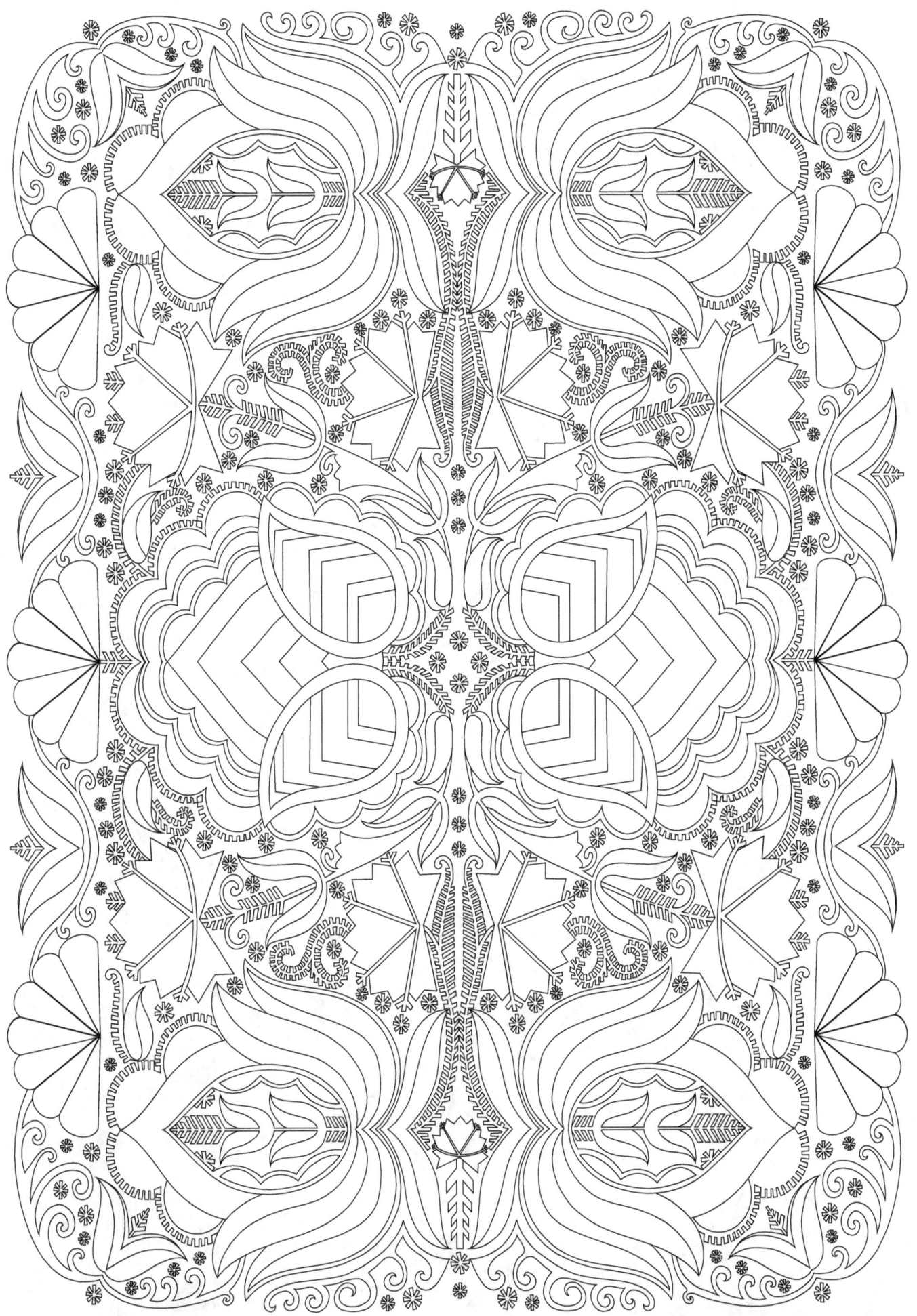

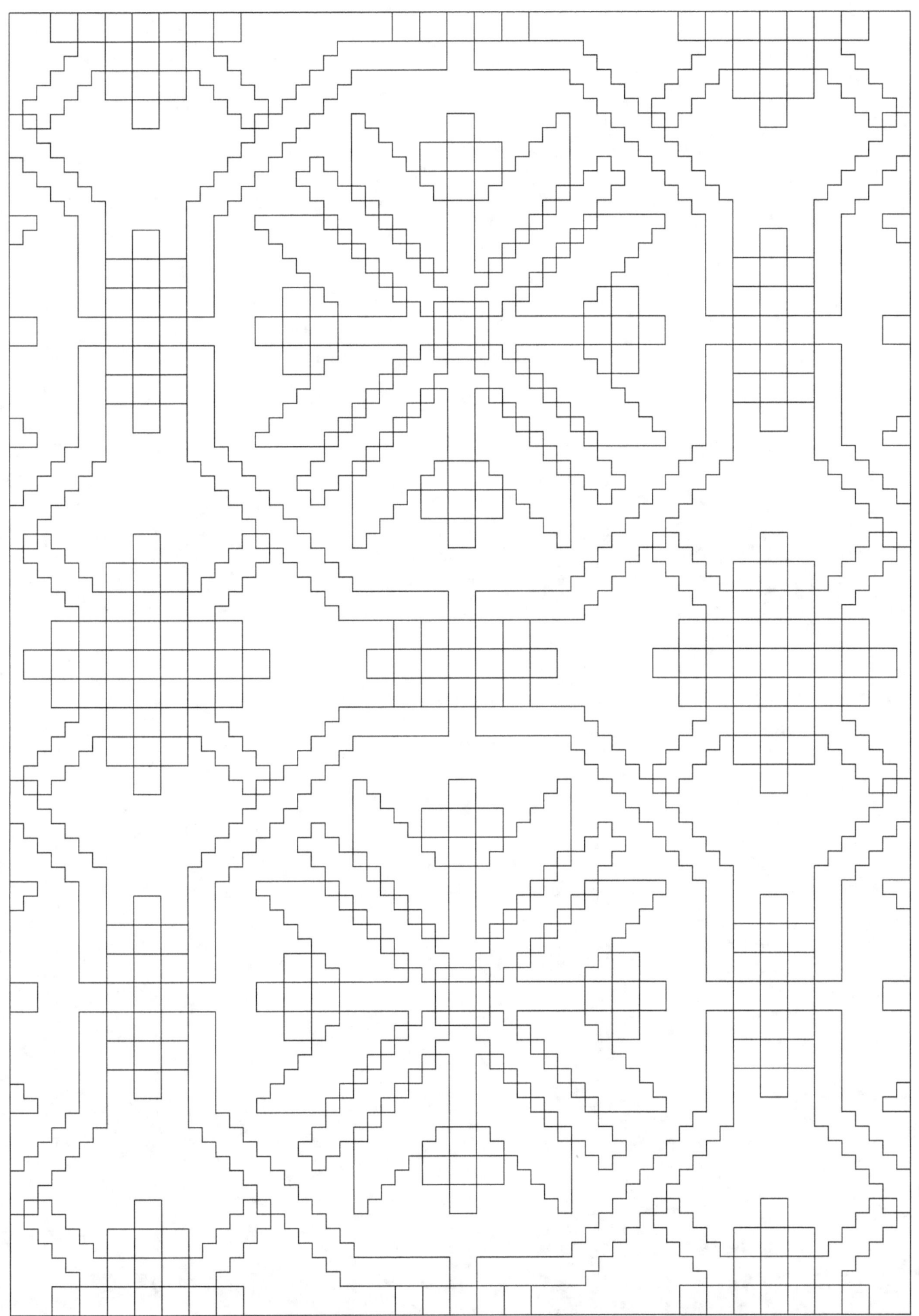

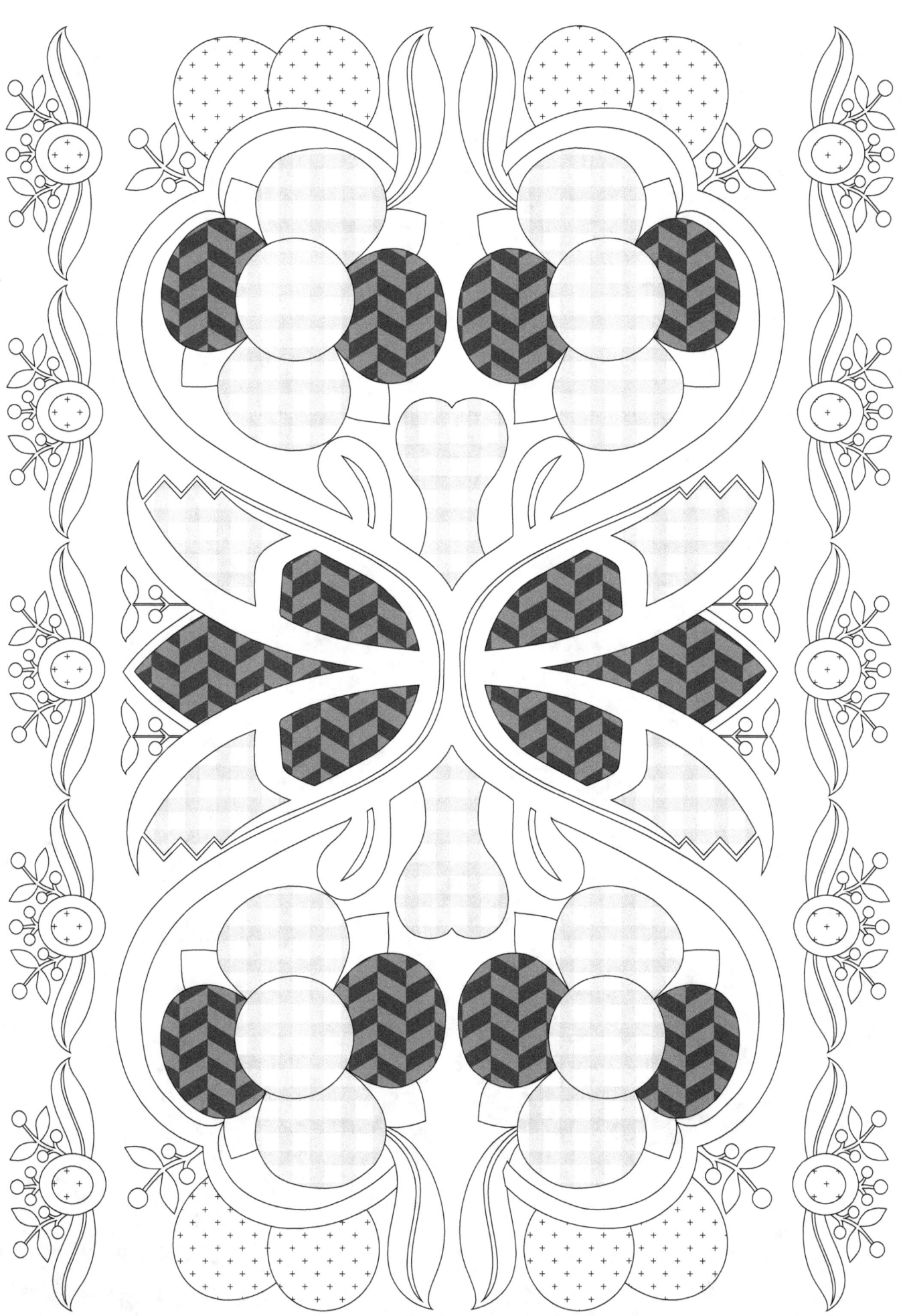

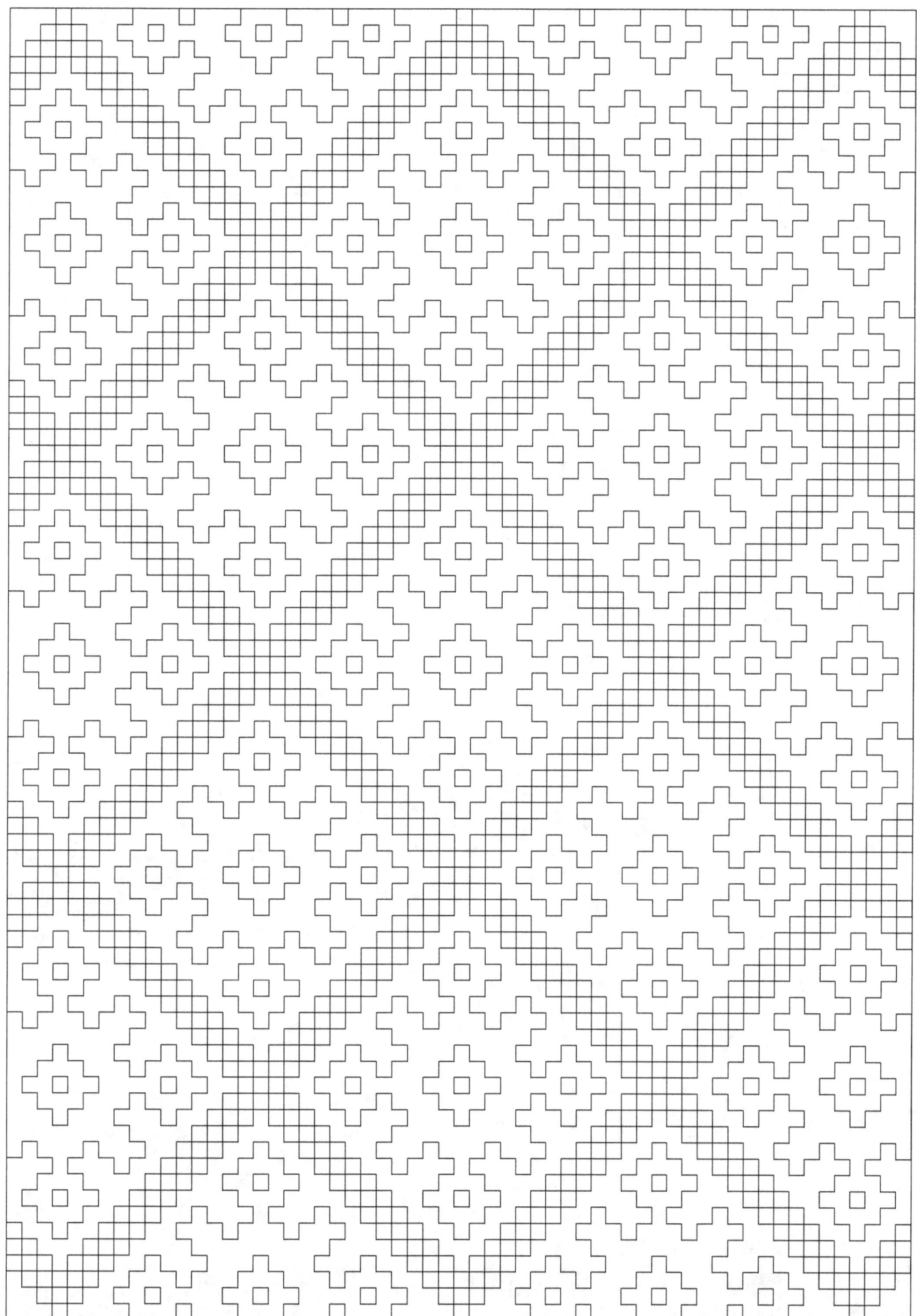

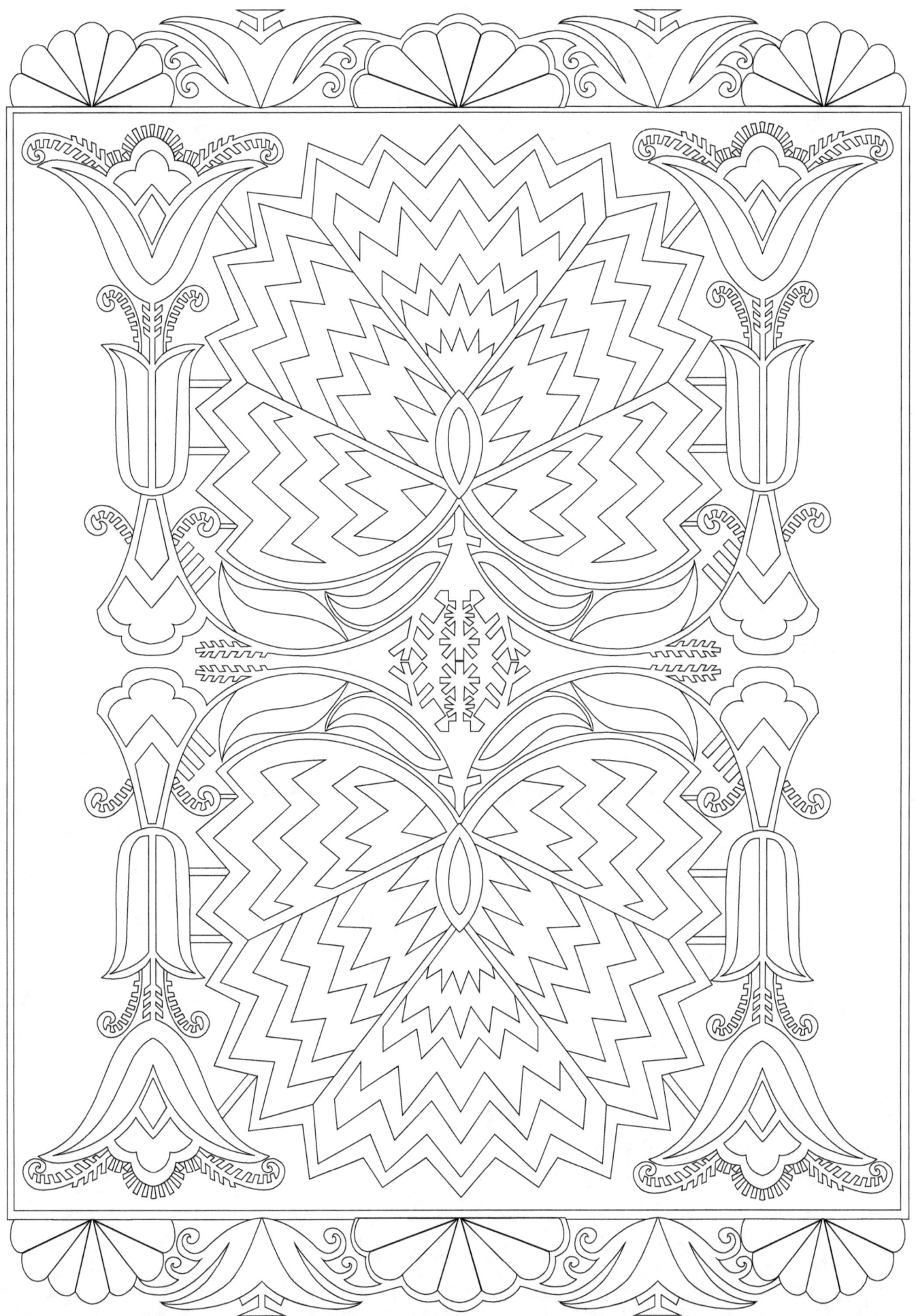

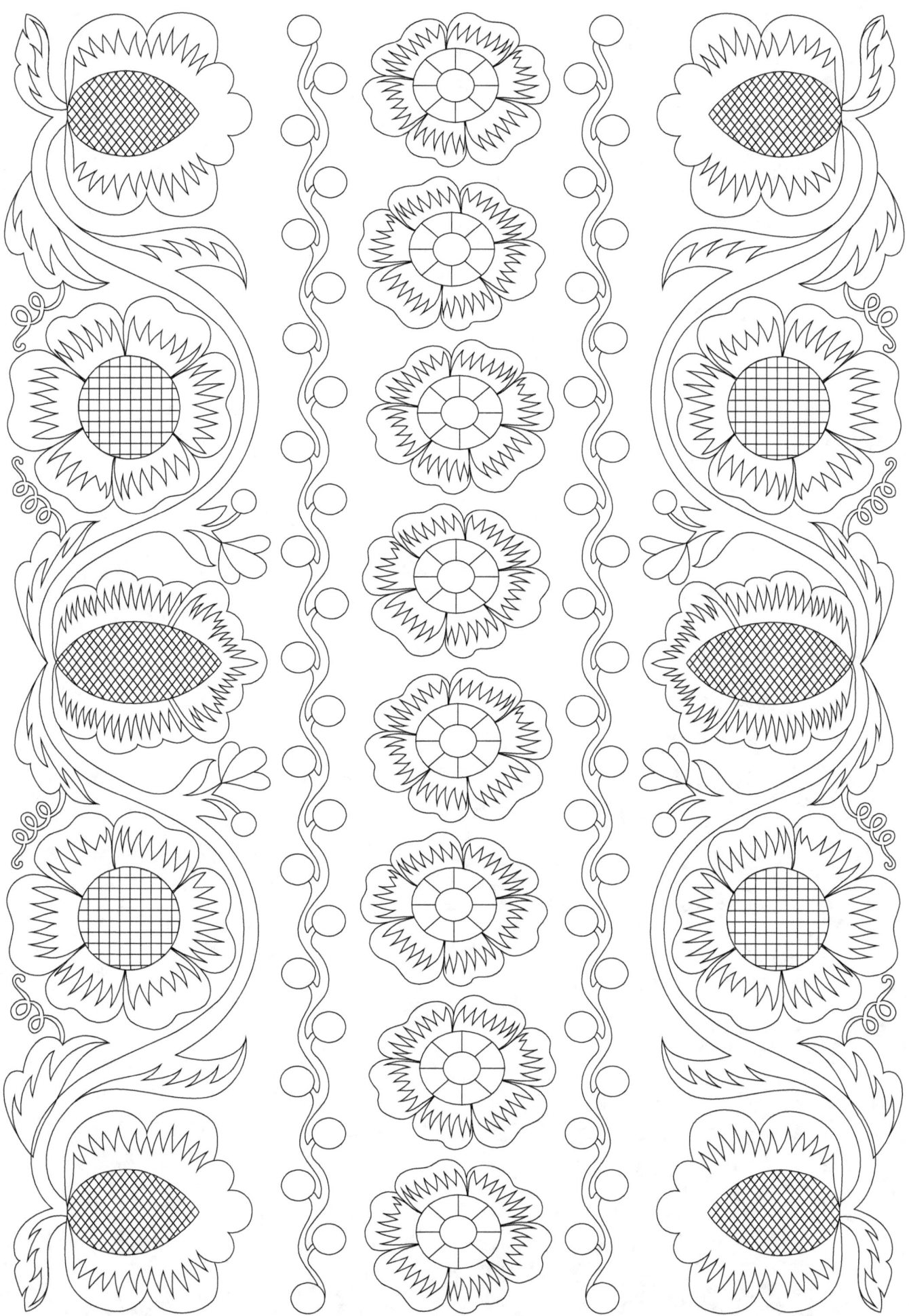

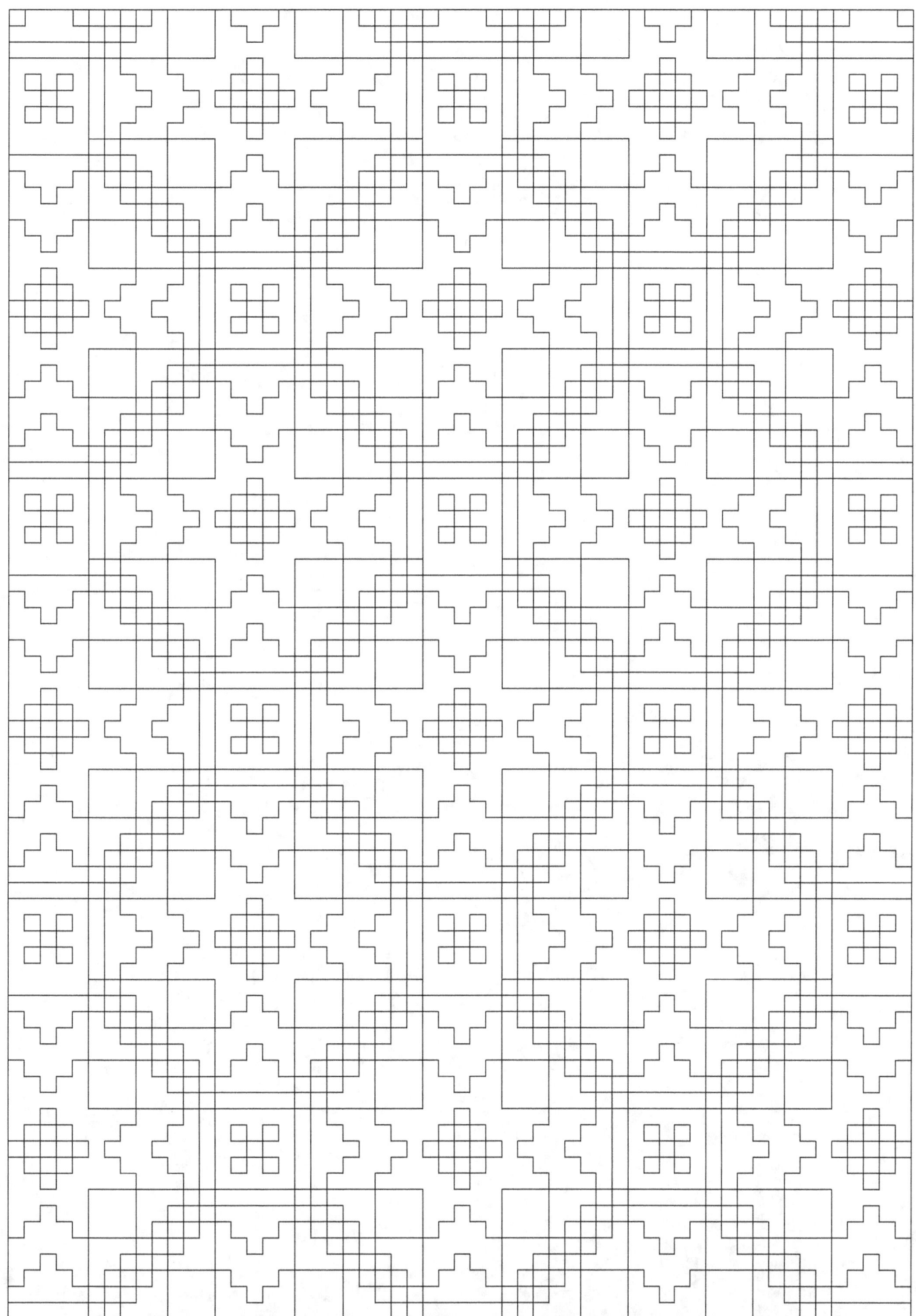

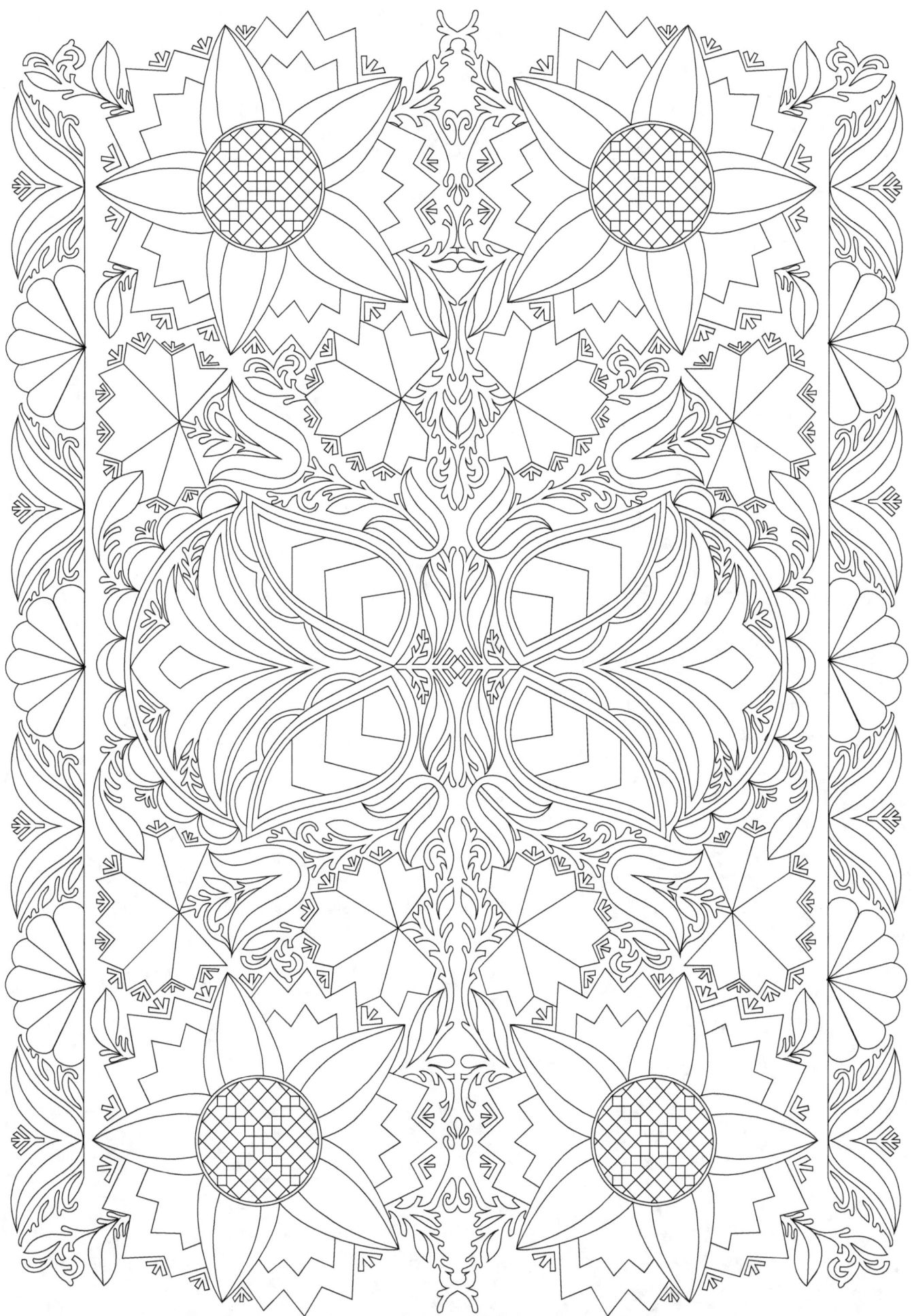

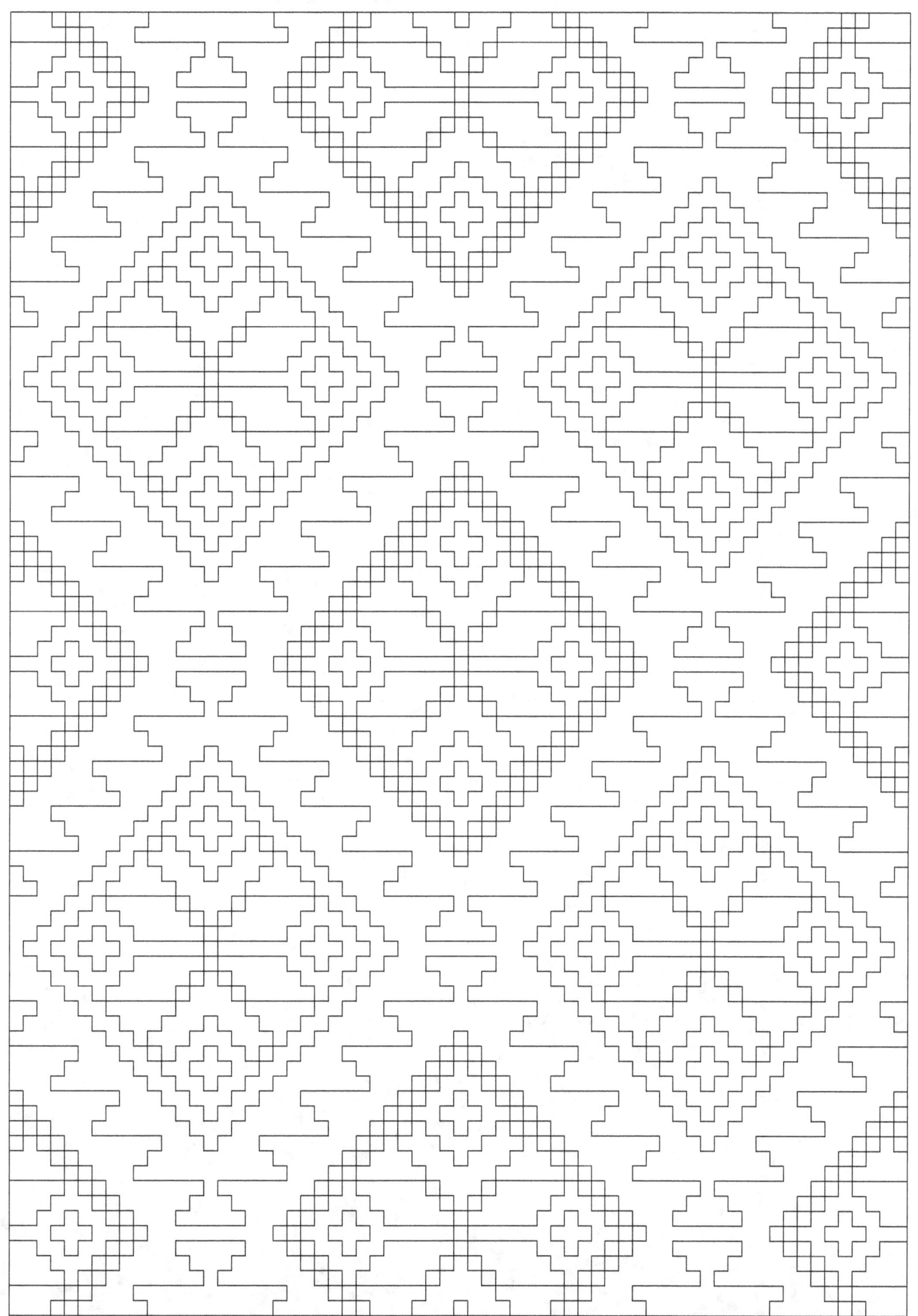

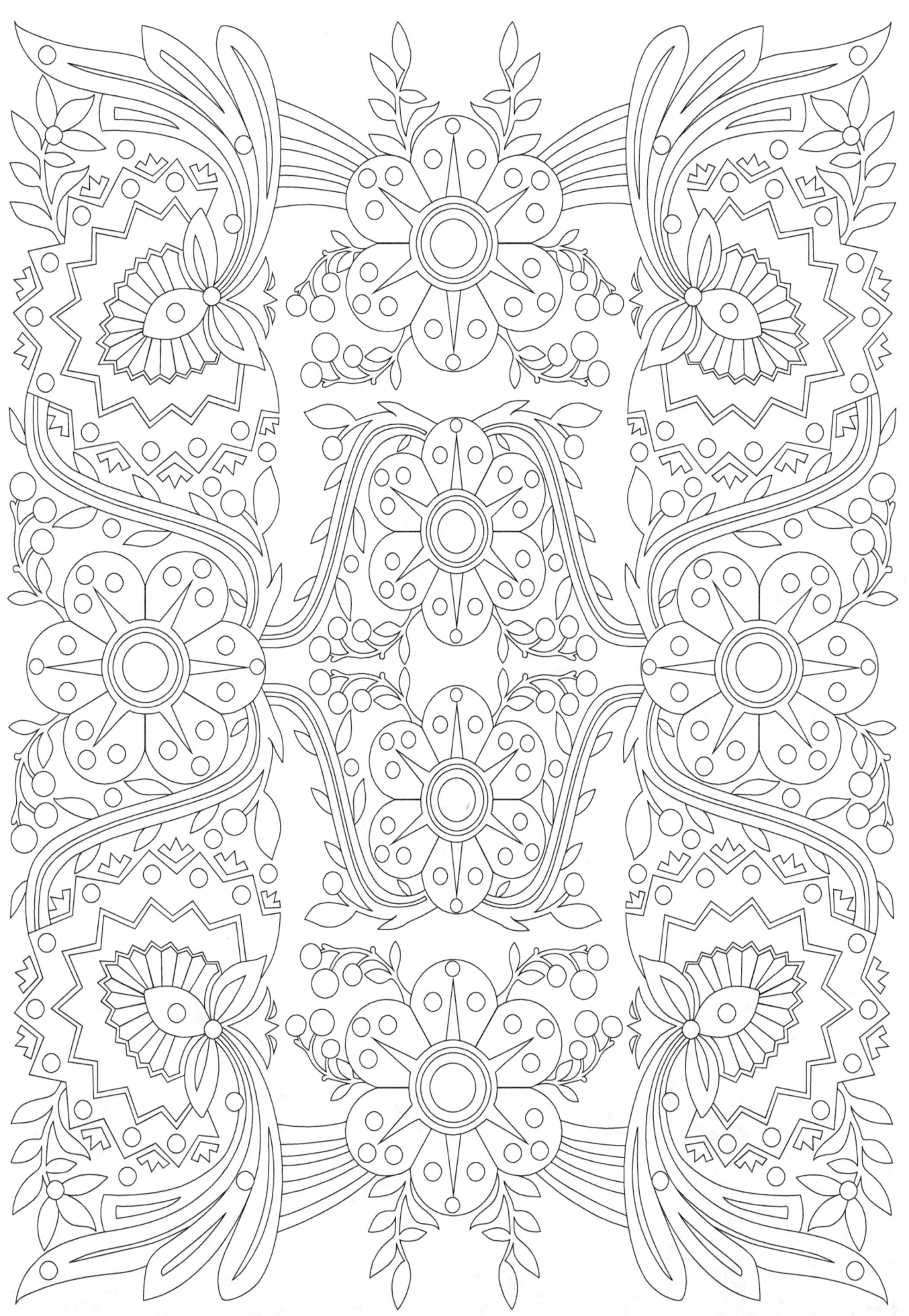

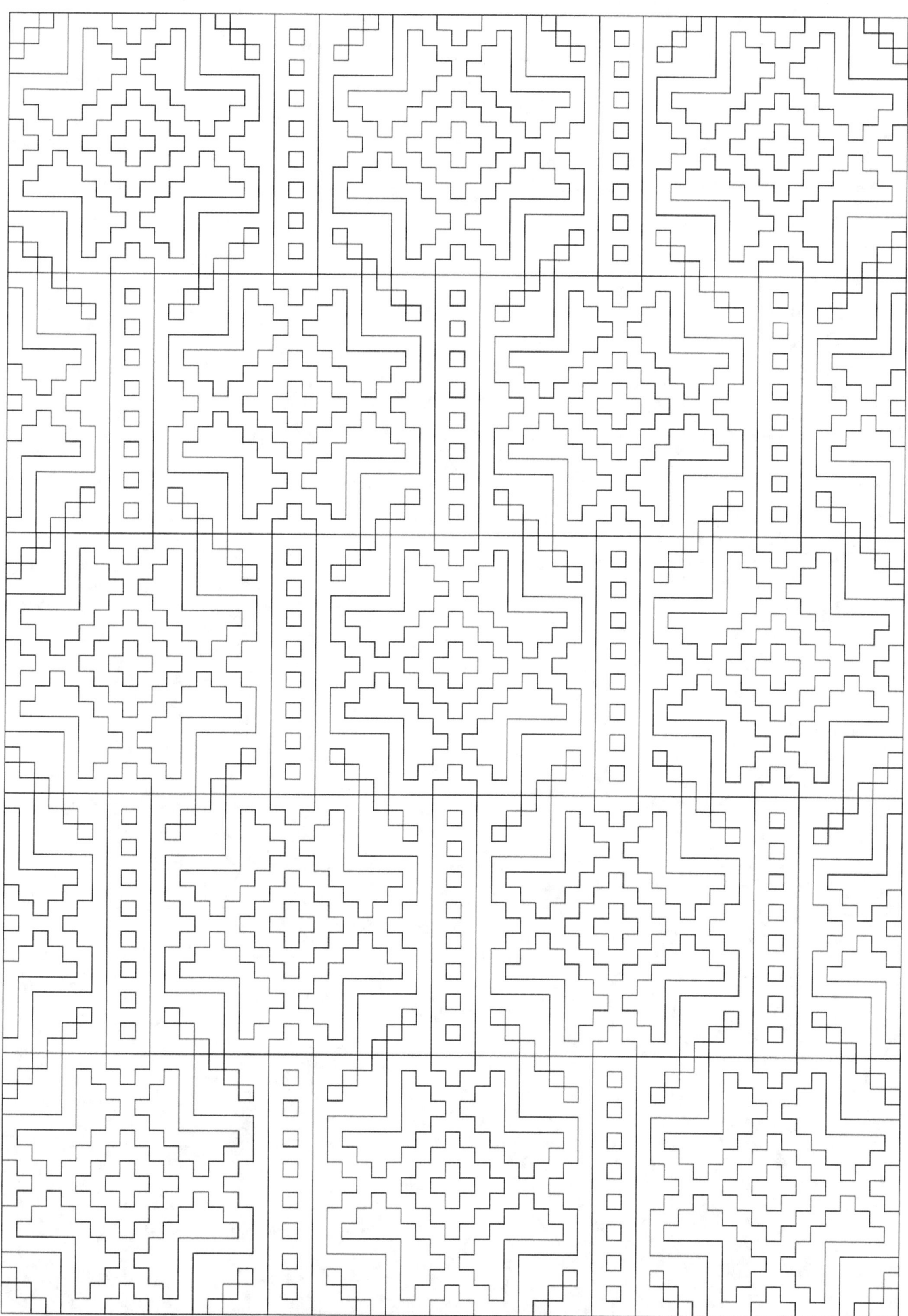

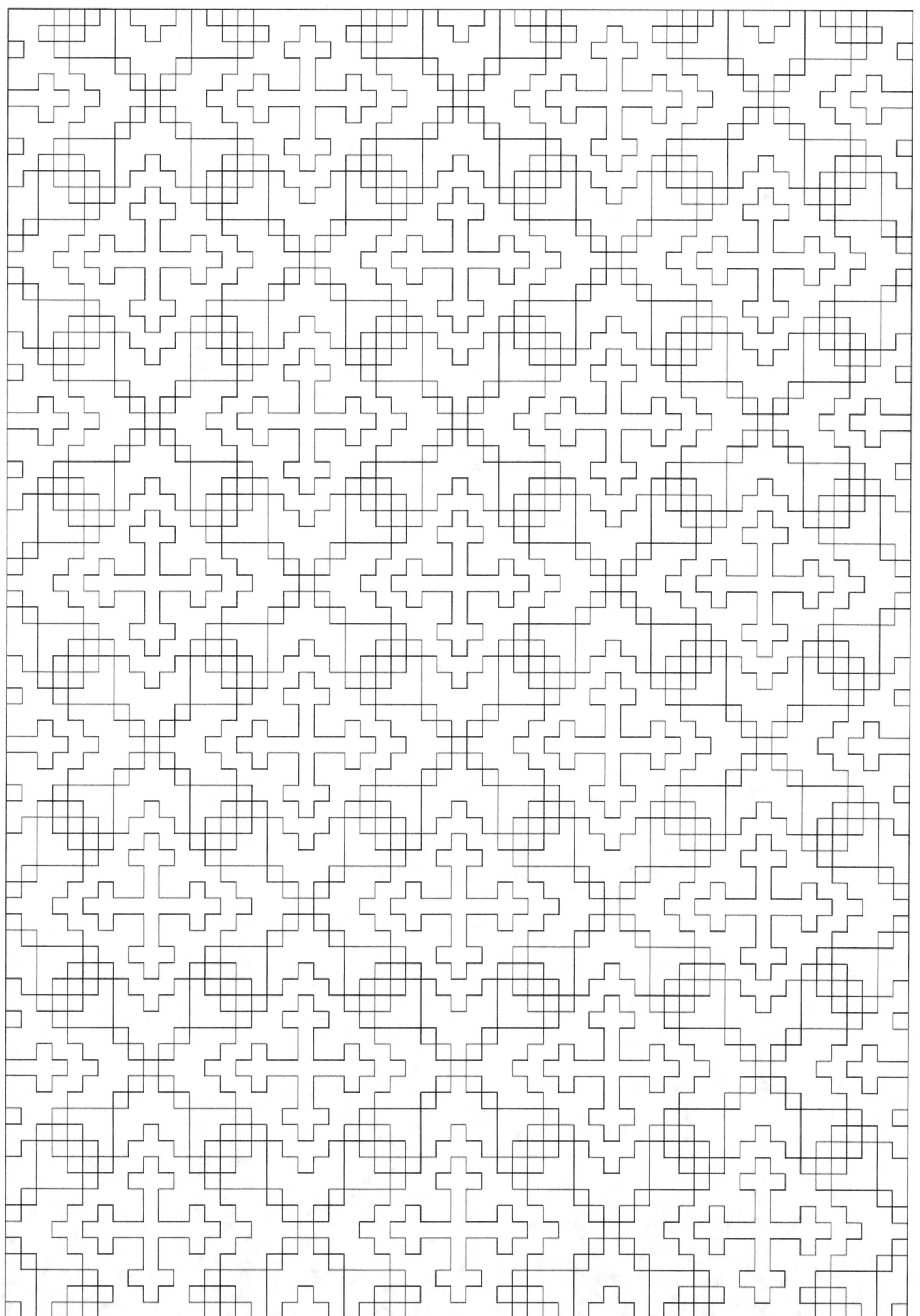

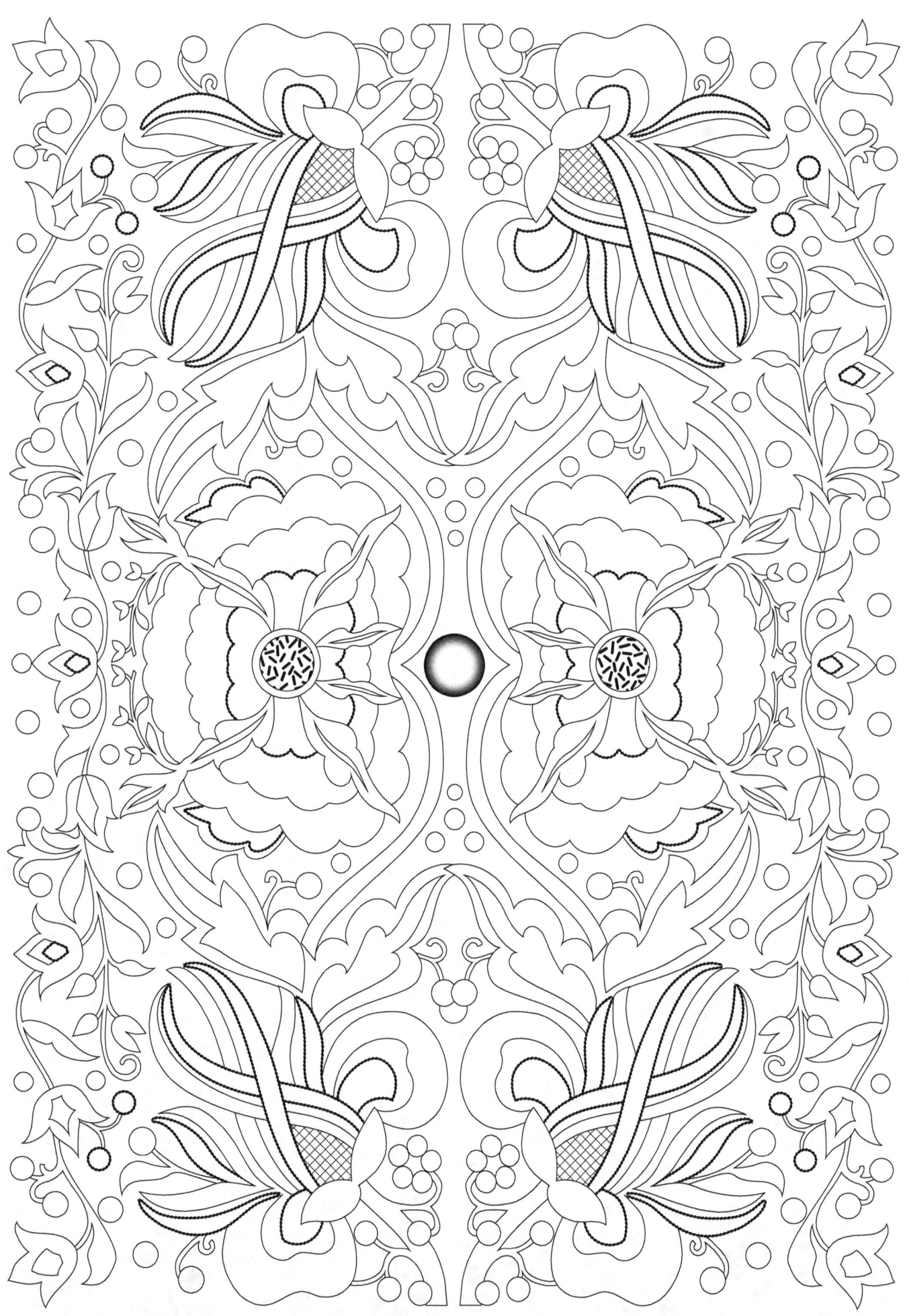

www.ingramcontent.com/pod-product-compliance
Lightning Source LLC
Chambersburg PA
CBHW081749220526
45468CB00008B/2309